Interruptions

Interruptions

God's Unexpected Opportunities

Joseph M. Stowell

MOODY PRESS
CHICAGO

ISBN: 0-8024-4743-0

1 3 5 7 9 10 8 6 4 2

Printed in the United States of America

Life would be an absolute pleasure . . . if it weren't for the interruptions.

I am usually awake before Martie. In those early hours of the morning, I enjoy having a little time to myself.

I hate to sound so unspiritual, but the first agenda in my day is not dropping to my knees by the side of my bed, but rather making my way sleepily to the kitchen to grab that big, heavy mug and fill it with Columbia's best.

With coffee in hand, I go to the living room and start the day with the Lord in prayer and His Word. I usually end up praying through my day, appointment by appointment.

From my living room chair in the pre-dawn, I am in full control of my life. Yet down deep inside there is the haunting thought that my day will most likely be savaged by the almost inevitable interruption or two or twenty.

Disruption is only a phone call away. From a small glitch to a major disaster, life has a way of being shattered by interruptions.

It was a day like most days in the office for me. Full of appointments, meetings, paperwork, correspondence, etc. That is, until 3:40 when someone burst through my door with a flushed face announcing that a gunman was holding staff and students hostage in our athletic center and had threatened to kill someone if his demands weren't met. I grabbed my coat and ran for the door, and as I made my way across the campus I noticed police cars and news vans. This interruption was certainly not the kind that one would look forward to.

Our campus is secured against this kind of danger, but it became apparent to me that no one or no place is ultimately safe from those who seek to do harm. I found myself standing on the sidewalk outside the building waiting and wondering if I would soon hear a shot that would signal the beginning of great measures of grief and sorrow to all of us on the campus and loved ones in far off places.

As the story unfolded there were about twenty-five of our students seated on the floor of the lobby, a faculty member being held as a human shield, two staff members on either side of the man who insisted he had a gun, and Chicago's hostage-crisis-trained police force poised behind pillars in the lobby with their guns aimed directly at the perpetrator of the crime. I stood traumatized on the sidewalk, processing all the possibilities that might grow out of this interruption in the minutes that stretched ahead of us. It was an interruption that was more than unwelcome. I wanted to resist it with everything within me. Yet I knew that above and beyond it there was a sovereign God whose sovereign oversight of our lives even includes interruptions as devastating as these.

Life has a way of interrupting our peace, our plans, our dreams, our health, our families, and our wealth. That all-time great philosopher, Dr. Seuss, puts life in perspective when he writes to children,

(handwritten annotations: "(?)", "wrong ownership", "only interruptions if we are the possessors !")

> You'll be on your way up!
> You'll be seeing great sights!
> You'll join the high flyers
>   who soar to great heights.
> You won't lag behind,
>   because you'll have the speed.
> You'll pass the whole gang
>   and you'll soon take the lead.
> Wherever you fly,
>   you'll be the best of the best.
> Wherever you go,
>   you will top all the rest.
>
> Except when you don't.
> Because sometimes, you won't.

7

I'm sorry to say so
But, sadly it's true
That bang-ups
And hang-ups
Can happen to you.

You can get all hung-up
In a pricke-ly perch.
And your gang will fly on.
You'll be left in a lurch.

You'll come down from the lurch
With an unpleasant bump.
And the chances are, then,
That you'll be in a slump.[1]

Dr. Seuss concludes, "And when you're in a slump, you're not in for much fun, unslumping yourself is not easily done!"

Simple, but profound. Life is like that. Sometimes the bumps and detours are small ones: a change of plans, an unexpected phone call, an unplanned conversation with a stranger, a traffic jam. Those interruptions, those frustrating intrusions into our orderly schedules, are annoying. At other times, however, life's interruptions can be devastating.

It is not so easy to shrug off interruptions when they involve the death of a loved one, the loss of a job, or the diagnosis of a life-threatening illness. These life-altering interruptions have the power to derail even the best-laid plans, to send us spiraling downward into an emotional slump.

Unexpected invasions of our well-ordered lives throw us off course. We struggle for answers, asking: "What is the purpose? What is God doing? Why has our life been turned in this strange direction?" Measures of despair wash our hearts and minds and erode hope.

It never seems to cross our minds that interruptions may very well be *God's unexpected opportunities to be specially used for purposes above and beyond ourselves.*

In Proverbs, King Solomon gives us this sage advice: "Many are the plans in a man's heart, but it is the Lord's purpose that prevails" (19:21). Solomon was right. In fact, if we know the divine potential in interruptions we may want to have a few now and then.

When our children were little, Martie and I enjoyed taking them on surprise trips. We would plan an outing and tell the children to get ready without giving them any clue as to our destination.

Do you think their reaction was dismay or fear? No, they were never traumatized by their lack of information. They never stubbornly folded their arms and said, "We're not going on this surprise trip unless you tell us all about it."

Instead, the prospect of a surprise trip sent our kids into a flurry of excitement, getting their coats and urging us out the door to get going. They were delighted at the prospect of what the trip would involve. They embraced the interruption because they trusted their parents.

Should we trust God less?

We tend to respond to interruptions with frustration, irritation, and, if it's serious enough, fear and doubt.

Hannah Whitall Smith, in her book *The Christian's Secret of a Happy Life,* points out, "You must remember that our God has all knowledge and all wisdom, and that therefore it is very possible He may guide you into paths wherein He knows great blessings are awaiting you, but which to the shortsighted human eyes around you seem sure to result in confusion and loss."[2]

What Smith is saying is that God's direction, His choices, may not make sense to us from an earthly perspective. But that does not mean that His plans are without purpose. Smith continues, "You must recognize the fact that God's thoughts are not as man's thoughts, nor His ways as man's ways, and that He who knows the ends of things from the beginning alone can judge of what the results of any course of action may be."

Let's think back a moment through the stretch of biblical history. Paging through the stories of the heroes of our faith, we realize that some of the greatest things God did through people's lives took place when He dramatically and unexpectedly interrupted their plans.

Ravaged by a Storm

Think of Noah. In a land where rain hardly ever, if ever, took place, God interrupted Noah's life and asked him to build a boat. Scripture tells us that "Noah was a righteous man, blameless among the people of his time, and he walked with God" (Genesis 6:9). Imagine Noah's surprise when faced with such an unusual request. Imagine what this interruption meant to his own plans and his own sense of identity as he became the laughingstock of all the locals. He must have looked heavenward and asked God, "What? You want me to do *what*?"

People who had thought of Noah with respect now thought he had lost his mind. At some 500 years of age, in the middle of desert land, Noah began construction on the world's largest boat. The Bible tells us, "Noah did all that the Lord commanded him."

And, when he was 600, the floods began. Because Noah was

faithful . . . because Noah obeyed God without question . . . because Noah honored God despite this unusual interruption . . . in the midst of terrible judgment upon the earth, God was able to use Noah to preserve a faithful group of people.

An Unexpected Move

Think back to more than two millennia before Christ was born. Abraham lived in the sophisticated, advanced culture of Ur of the Chaldees. Abram, as he was then called, was a wealthy seventy-five-year-old man. Through a lifetime of hard work, he had acquired flocks and herds and an extensive staff to run his household. In our day and age, Abram and his wife, Sarai, would have been preparing to move to Florida and retire in a lavish Palm Beach condominium.

Abram's life was running smoothly until God interrupted it and said, "Leave your country, your people and your father's household and go to the land I will show you" (Genesis 12:1). In so many words, God said, "Abram, pack up, leave it all behind, I want you to go on a trip. And by the way, don't ask Me where you're going. Just start walking, and I'll tell you when you get there."

Abram did not question God's plans or God's promises. Instead, acting on the promise of God, he yielded to the interruption and started out with his family to travel to a foreign land, a land still occupied by strangers.

God interrupted Abram's life for a great purpose: to go to a special place to begin a nation. One day that nation would bring forth the Messiah that we might know the liberation of redemption. Abram was told the purpose (Genesis 12:2–3), but neither the location nor how it would happen. Yet he trusted God and packed up his possessions and left with his wife and nephew for the land of Canaan.

A Journey into the Pit

Think of Joseph. He was Jacob's favorite son: a seventeen year old who was bright, handsome, and dedicated to God. Jacob was so proud of his son that he made him a beautiful robe as a sign of honor. This did not sit well with Joseph's brothers.

In a fit of jealousy and rage, his brothers stripped him of his robe, threw him in an empty cistern, and sold him into slavery for twenty shekels of silver. Joseph's promising future had come to a screeching halt. *What could God be thinking? How could He let evil plans affect my life?*

Those certainly could have been Joseph's thoughts. But they were not. He yielded to God's interruption.

Through all the twists and turns in Egypt—understood only to the One overseeing the interruption—Joseph was catapulted into Egyptian leadership, rescued his family and nation from a great famine, and, in doing so, preserved the line that would eventually lead to the Messiah.

Joseph, realizing the divine hand of God in his life, said to his brothers when they came begging his forgiveness, "Do not be angry with yourselves for selling me here, because it was to save lives that God sent me ahead of you. . . . God sent me ahead of you to preserve for you a remnant on earth and to save your lives by a great deliverance. So then, it was not you who sent me here, but God" (Genesis 45:5, 7–8).

These were not Joseph's plans, but neither were they the plans of his brothers. Joseph's life had been interrupted for great purposes beyond himself.

Fire in the Desert

Nearly four hundred years after Joseph and the descendants of Jacob (Israel) had settled in Egypt, God chose Moses to deliver His people from the bonds of slavery. No one could have felt less qualified than Moses. He was busy caring for the flock of his father-in-law, Jethro. He took the sheep to the far side of the desert, to the mountain of God named Horeb. Tending sheep is a job that demands concentration, but it isn't high on the list of exciting career moves. It is monotonous, steadfast, and solitary.

Suddenly, on the back side of the wilderness, a bush becomes aflame with the presence of God, from which God says, "I want you to be a leader of My people." Not only that, but God had chosen Moses to approach Pharaoh, a tyrannical ruler who had taken His entire people into captivity, to demand that the nation of Israel be set free.

It was an interruption that was a threat to his secure, even serene, style of living. Amazed at this turn of events, Moses replies, "Who am I, that I should go to Pharaoh and bring the Israelites out of Egypt?" (Exodus 3:11). But God simply says, "I will be with you" (v. 12). So, Moses goes. And, because of Moses' willing surrender to the interruption, the people of Israel are delivered from slavery. Through the ages, Israel's seed is kept safe to someday produce the promised Messiah.

Losing Everything

No one's interruptions were quite as devastating as those faced by Job. A righteous man, Job lost everything—his wife, his family, his health, his livelihood.

Job lived in the land of Uz. He was a wealthy man, with seven sons and three daughters. Scripture tells us that he owned seven thousand sheep, three thousand camels, five hundred yoke of oxen, and five hundred donkeys; he also had a large number of servants. He was a great man, well known among all of the people of the East.

But that is not all we know about Job. We also know that he "was blameless and upright; he feared God and shunned evil" (Job 1:1).

Why then was it all taken away? The book of Job tells of Satan's attack on Job's life. Satan, wanting to defame God before all the heavenly host, tests Job's devotion to God. He strips him of everything that is dear to him. His children are killed, his wealth is destroyed, even his health is affected. Job's faith in God is put to the ultimate test.

When everything seems lost, Job asks God, "Why?"

His answer?

God's ways are not man's ways. God's understanding and His purpose are beyond our human, limited comprehension. Yet, while realizing that, we know that we can trust Him. For what shall we say of Jesus Christ, whose own eternal existence was abruptly interrupted as the eternal decree sent Him here to this fallen place for thirty-three years to be misunderstood, maligned, and ultimately martyred on a cruel instrument of ancient torture? All for an obvious purpose that would cast a victorious ray of light down through the centuries to my life and to yours and to all who follow us who will come and embrace the Cross.

What I find interesting is that throughout biblical history when people have surrendered to the interruption and said, "God, I am willing to let You use this interruption to transition me to Your intended purposes," God has used the interruption to accomplish things far beyond themselves.

And it can't go unnoticed that God knows what He is doing. As He was with Joseph, He is with us through the interruption. And like Job he restricts and prohibits any interruption that He can't use to His gain and glory.

Do you ever wonder what it would have been like if Abraham had said, "I don't do trips," or if Noah had said, "I don't do boats," or if Moses had said, "I don't do crowds"? Think of what it would have been like if Joseph had said, "I don't do rescue operations in Egypt," if Job had said, "I don't do sorrow," or if Christ had said, "I don't do crosses." Where would we be today?

It seems to me that there is a greater issue involved here. We must ask ourselves: Are we willing to let the interruptions in our lives be used for things beyond ourselves—to be used for *His* glory, His gain, and our good? Are we willing to stop resisting life's interruptions and to welcome them as God's unscheduled opportunities?

Some of us have experienced devastating interruptions in our lives. The key is our response. Will we be crushed under the cascading weight of frustration, anger, or bitterness or be willing to say, "God, I accept this interruption as a way that You can use me for something significant beyond myself"?

An Unplanned Pregnancy

Perhaps the most instructive pattern for a productive response to interruptions is found in the upheaval that came to a young couple early in the New Testament. Their willingness to surrender literally changed history. In Matthew chapter 1, verse 18, we read, "This is how the birth of Jesus Christ came about. His mother Mary was pledged to be married to Joseph, but before they came together, she was found to be with child."

For Mary this experience was a devastating interruption. To be unmarried and expecting a child in that culture was the ultimate shame and humiliation.

The interruption was equally devastating for Joseph. His plans were radically changed when the angel of the Lord appeared to him in a dream and said, "Joseph son of David, do not be afraid to take Mary home as your wife, because what is conceived in her is from the Holy Spirit. She will give birth to a son, and you are to give him the name Jesus, because he will save his people from their sins" (vv. 20–21).

Matthew adds the editorial comment, "All this took place to fulfill what the Lord had said through the prophet: 'The virgin will be with child and will give birth to a son, and they will call him Immanuel'—which means, 'God with us' " (vv. 22–23).

So, Joseph surrendered to the interruption. "He did what the angel of the Lord had commanded him and took Mary home as his wife. But he had no union with her until she gave birth to a son. And he gave him the name Jesus" (vv. 24–25).

How Will I Tell My Parents?

Stop for a moment and weigh the massive implications of this interruption. Consider the impact of this unexpected event on the life of Mary. She was probably a young girl, sixteen or seventeen years of age. Mary was betrothed to Joseph, a commitment not unlike our engagement period, only far more serious in Jewish law. The betrothal period was a covenant time when the couple promised themselves to one another. It was the official prelude to the great and sacred Jewish marriage ceremony.

The worst thing you could do during the betrothal period would be to be found with child. It was a Jewish shame beyond repair. Think about the fact that this young girl did not live in the huge metropolis of Jerusalem where she could escape to the other side of town and begin a new life.

Mary lived in the backwater village of Nazareth. A little country town. One of those towns where everybody knows each other, where everybody knows each other's business. In these little country towns Jewish law was firmly embraced. In the midst of this setting Mary, a young unmarried girl, was found expecting a baby. This was a devastating interruption in her life. What would she tell her mother? What would you tell your mother? I can just hear her saying, "Mom, it's an angel thing; you've got to understand that, really!" You and I both know that would not be an acceptable explanation.

Joseph's Dilemma

Imagine the fear Mary felt at telling Joseph. Before God revealed to him the right perspective, he must surely have felt dreadfully betrayed. Mary, this young, tender Jewish girl whom he has loved and committed himself to has betrayed his trust. How could she do that kind of damage to him personally, to their love, to their future, and to his reputation in their hometown? He would be the only guy in town who knew that he was not the father of this child.

Think of Joseph's business. Joseph had a little carpentry shop. In a little town like that, who would do business with a guy like Joseph? No one would want a sign that said "Kitchens by Joseph" staked in the front yard. His reputation was virtually destroyed. Personally, emotionally, and financially, this was a devastating interruption both to Joseph and to Mary.

What I find fascinating is that this young couple takes us to school on how to transition even the worst interruptions of our lives into God's intended purposes. Joseph's response is especially motivating and instructive.

Unfortunately, Joseph doesn't get much publicity at Christmas. About the only thing we think about Joseph is that he is the guy leading a donkey to Bethlehem. But Matthew is writing about Christ the King, so he directs our attention to Joseph. Joseph is a descendant of the line of David, the line that gives Christ the earthly credentials of His kingship.

Joseph's response provides the key. Through Joseph's example, we learn how to accept our interruptions and transition them to God's intended purposes.

The pattern for success emerges from two realities in Joseph's life: his *personhood* and his *perspective.* Interruptions will always test what kind of people we are. They will either reveal impatience, anxieties, anger, and self-centeredness or our undaunted commitment to responding righteously regardless of the cost.

In Matthew 1:19, we learn that Joseph was "a righteous man." The word "righteous" in Scripture basically means doing what is right, correct, and according to the standard of God. God is a righteous God. All that He is and all that He does is always correct. His standard is always true. A righteous person is one whose life is consistent with the standards of God.

Proverbs 4:18 tells us, "The path of the righteous is like the first gleam of dawn, shining ever brighter till the full light of day." Psalm 15:2 speaks of the righteous man: "He whose walk is blameless and who does what is righteous, who speaks the truth from his heart."

In our generation, as perhaps was true in Joseph's, it is not an easy task to be righteous. Our culture gives us a whole menu of choices and standards to which we can conform. You should do what you want to do, do what is right in your own eyes, do what is politically correct. Unfortunately, that is usually not what God would call righteous.

It is possible to be politically correct, but incorrect before God. We can be correct before our friends, but incorrect before God. We can be correct according to our own rationalization and our own desires and our own plans, maybe even according to our own personal standards, but incorrect before God.

A young unmarried woman today, faced with an unplanned pregnancy, would probably ask herself, "What is best for *me*?" "What do *I* want to do?" "Should *I* keep this baby? How will it change *my* life?" The father might say to her, "Why don't you get rid of it?" "*I* don't have time for this right now." "This isn't what *I* want for *my* life!"

When the focus of our life centers around our own desires, our decision making inevitably becomes self-centered and introverted. Selfishness is not righteousness.

A righteous person at each intersection of life steps back from the immediate circumstances, from his or her immediate self-oriented response, and measures what is the right thing to do before God. *What would God do? What is righteous at this moment?*

It is then that the righteous person brings his life into conformity with God's standard. It is a definite pulling away from ourselves and toward God that results in righteousness. It is not natural, it is not always easy, but it is right and pure and true before God.

Joseph was that kind of a person. When the interruption came into his life he did not ask himself, "How will this inconvenience my life?", but, "What would be right to do before God?"

Joseph was an obedient man. As author Walter Wangerin explains, "He obeyed the word of God, whether written in the laws of Moses or uttered in dreams by angels. He obeyed, and obedience made a marriage where there might have been divorce. Obedience saved his son from Herod's hatred. Joseph's obedience took him to Egypt and then again to the security of Nazareth."[3]

Unfortunately, when my life is interrupted my first response is not always obedience. I don't always make that quick transition to consider what is the right thing to do before God. To be perfectly honest, I usually think about my own rights, plans, interests, and feelings that have been trampled by this interruption.

The residuals of my fallenness propose a whole litany of options. Righteous behavior too often is not the foremost thought on my mind.

But Joseph points us in the right direction. What would a righteous person do in these circumstances? Joseph has two options. Jewish law said that a girl who betrayed her betrothed, a woman who had been unfaithful, should be taken outside the city gates and stoned to death. Or, the second and gentler option, according to Jewish law, would be to privately take her to the local priests and have a rabbi in a private ceremony, with no public announcement, sign a bill of divorcement. That is the option Joseph chose.

What I find fascinating in this text, more fascinating than the fact that Joseph chose a righteous option, is his attitude in his response to this difficult situation. It is true that most of us wouldn't have wanted to haul our betrothed one out to be stoned. Maybe we would have said, "Let's do the other thing." But it's the motivation of his heart that stuns me. The text records Joseph's response. It says, "Not wanting to disgrace her."

Compassion with a Capital "C"

What kind of man was Joseph? That phrase gives us rich clues to his character. Not wanting to disgrace her showed that he was clearly a man of compassion.

Joseph was more concerned about Mary's needs in this moment than about his own. We must remember that he doesn't know the whole story yet. As far as Joseph is concerned, Mary has been unfaithful to him in the worst possible way. She has betrayed him, depreciated his business, and wrecked his reputation.

Most men wouldn't react like Joseph. I doubt that many of us would have said, "Now the first thing I don't want to do is disgrace her." In our human, self-centered response, most of us would look out for our own interests, wanting everyone to know the "true story," getting ourselves out of the pit at her expense. We may not even be alert to the ramifications on the other person, because our attention is so riveted on ourselves.

Looking Out for Others

In this case, though, Joseph's righteousness was revealed in his depth of compassion toward the one who had hurt him. When his life was interrupted, his immediate response became, "How can I do what is best for this one who has brought the interruption?"

How strange that seems. Interruptions violate our rights. Unexpected changes in our plans reveal us as dreadfully self-focused. Yet, God calls us to just the opposite. We are to ask ourselves, *What would be right before God? What would be the best thing I could do about this interruption that has come into my life?*

A couple of months ago, Martie and I were on a rather extended ministry trip that involved several segments to our journey. We were in and out of planes, and every plane was packed with people.

We felt like sardines traveling in aluminum cans. On every leg of the journey we had terrible seating assignments: middle seats, back seats. But on the last leg of the journey, we looked at our boarding passes and, to our delight, found that we had the best seats on the plane. We couldn't believe it. We had the front aisle seats in the coach section.

If you travel much, you know that the aisle seats let you lean out in the aisle, providing a little more room. We couldn't have been happier with our assigned seats. Martie would be in one aisle seat and I would sit in the one across from her, seats 5 C and D.

Arriving late to the airport, we hurried to board the plane. The flight attendant, checking tickets, asked us, "By the way, where are you sitting?"

"5 C and D," I said.

"Oh, *you're* the folks in 5 C and D," she said.

Her statement had a foreboding ring to it. *Why was she looking at us like that?* "We have a mother on board with two children. The two children are in 5 E and F, and strangely, she's been assigned several rows back on the window. She was wondering if whoever had 5 D would be willing to switch with her, so that she could sit with her kids."

The flight attendant went on to say, "We have an eighty-nine-year-old woman who is coming to get on the plane. We just got a call that she is being brought here in a wheelchair right now and she is in the middle seat next to that mother back there, and we thought maybe it would be better if she could sit in 5 C, if you'd be willing to change."

This was not a welcomed inter-ruption. Suddenly I became very pro-tective about seats 5 C and D. Didn't we have rights to those seats? Certainly, we deserved them! We needed space and comfort after our long, busy trip.

My first impulse was to say, "No, we want to keep our seats." I was sure that the elderly lady would do quite well sitting back there. Martie would take good care of the kids. Everything would be just fine.

But I knew what I had to do. I knew that we had to stop for a minute and ask ourselves, "What would be the right thing to do here? What would Christ do in a moment like this? How could we measure up to His righteousness? And what would be the compassionate thing to do?"

We needed to move from our own standards and expectations to the standard of God and turn our focus from ourselves to others. The demanding self-centered nature kicked and screamed, yet we knew what we had to do. The Holy Spirit was like a cattle prod as He pushed us back several rows and away from the aisle. We took our places, and I spent the rest of the trip with the back of the headrest in front of me pushed squarely in my face.

I have to tell you that I have no idea what God's intended purpose was in that interruption. I wish I could finish this story by saying that, as a result of our righteous, compassionate response, God did a phenomenal thing. I wish the story ended with the person sitting next to me asking to be told the way of salvation or something like that.

I don't know what God's purpose was. Maybe God did some things I don't know about. Maybe somebody who was going back to Chicago had heard of Moody Bible Institute and recognized me. Maybe that person was watching to see what God's people would do in a moment like this.

But the issue is not God's final intended purposes, because we do not always know what those purposes are. The issue at hand was our response to the situation, our faithfulness. We are to respond with righteous compassion regardless. It is God's business to write the last chapter.

Joseph understood that, and he applied it even when interrupted with a deep offense. His response is not unlike Christ, who felt compassion for me when I was so offensive to Him with my sin. How often, in my personal frustrations, do I fail to remember that Jesus Christ was willing to endure the ultimate interruption, to leave the perks of paradise, come here, and die on the cross for me?

Joseph was a righteous man, a man of obedience and compassion. The lesson he teaches us is profound. Joseph was the right kind of person, but he did not have a full perspective on the situation. According to what he knew, he only had two options: stone his fiancée or put her away privately.

Expanded Perspectives

Limited information always leads to limited conclusions. You know that, don't you? It is not unlike the Texas rancher who was in Germany on an agricultural consulting tour. Stopping by a small farm, he asked the farmer, "How big is your place?"

The German farmer said, "Oh, it is not real big. It is about a mile this way and a mile this way and a mile this way." Turning to the Texas rancher, he asked, "How big is your place?"

The Texan answered, "Oh, I don't know how to tell you this. Let's see. If I get in my pickup truck when the sun comes up, and if I drive all day long, when the sun goes down I'm still on my ranch."

The German farmer smiled, nodded, and said, "Oh, I know, I had a pickup truck like that once myself."

If you have the wrong perspective, your conclusions will be faulty. Limited information always brings limited conclusions. That is where Joseph was. What he needed to do was to have God come along and give him an expanded perspective on the situation.

Joseph was the right kind of person who embraced the right perspectives from God. Then, he followed through with the right response, conforming his life to God's will and surrendering to the interruption.

In the text we read, "But after he had considered this, an angel of the Lord appeared to him in a dream" (Matthew 1:20).

Through an angel, God revealed His divine perspective on this interruption. Today, we have another source for understanding life's interruptions. We have the objective, clear Word of God, from cover to cover. Thankfully, there is a perspective in this Book for every interruption that comes into our lives.

When you search the Word, God will lead you to His revealed perspective and give you enough information to respond correctly. But Joseph did not have the completed text of Scripture. God chose to expand his perspectives in a dream.

God revealed His perspective to Joseph in three life-changing points of view. The first thing God did to change his perspective was to give Joseph *an option he'd never thought of before.* Verse 20 says, "An angel of the Lord appeared to him in a dream and said, 'Joseph son of David, do not be afraid to take Mary home as your wife.'"

What? How could he marry the woman who was bringing him the ultimate shame? He'd never considered that option. Imagine your response if somebody came into your life and interrupted it by offending you in a deep, hurtful way. Quickly, a whole range of options would fill your mind.

Perhaps you would think, *I don't get mad, I get even.* Or maybe you would give that person the silent treatment, getting your revenge with a disdainful glance. You might choose to manipulate and try to control the situation to keep from being vulnerable again. Or perhaps you would lash out in anger. If the interruption was deep enough, bitterness might overshadow your choices.

If you were feeling particularly vengeful, you might go public with what that person had done and try to wreck his or her reputation. File a lawsuit. Blast the person with a scathing editorial in the local newspaper.

In those first moments after the interruption occurs, a whole range of options fills our minds, competing for attention. But God has given options we've never dreamed of.

For instance, in Matthew 5, verse 44, Jesus says, "Love your enemies and pray for those who persecute you."

Through these dramatically clear words, God brings a whole new perspective and a brand-new option. It is our choice whether to surrender to that perspective. Are we willing to allow the situation to be used toward God's intended purpose?

For each of us, there will be times when the interruptions of life push us into the ditch. You are traveling along life's road and everything is wonderful—and then suddenly you get a letter from your banker or a slip to come in and see your boss. Maybe it is as simple as turning the key of your car to find a dead battery. Maybe it is as devastating as receiving unwelcome news at a routine doctor's appointment.

There you are, lying in the ditch of life, and the embittered sense of being cheated and unjustly treated starts flowing through you. It is at that point that God's Word gives a brand-new option that revolutionizes your perspective.

James 1:2–3 says, "Consider it pure joy, my brothers, whenever you face trials of many kinds, because you know that the testing of your faith develops perseverance." Consider it joy? Even when life rolls you into the ditch?

Now I have to stop and say that this new option does not teach us that we are to love the pain. God does not call us to become spiritual masochists. We are not to say, "Oh Lord, I love it when You and I get in the ditch. Could we do the ditch thing again tomorrow?"

That is not what James is saying. The text says that you count it a thing of joy because you know that if God has permitted this in your life, He is using it to refine you and shape you and perfect you to make you more efficient and more effective. What is happening in your life is for your good and for His gain and His glory.

That is what the writer to the Hebrews says of Jesus Christ. At the beginning of chapter 12, after recounting the stories of the many heroes of the faith, he tells of our Savior, Jesus Christ. "Let us fix our eyes on Jesus, the author and perfecter of our faith, who for the joy set before him endured the cross." He went to the Cross for the joy that was set before Him . . . on the *other* side of the Cross, for what God would do *through* the Cross. Jesus Christ's example gives us a whole new perspective on interruptions.

Divine Purposes

It is not the interruption itself, but what God will accomplish through the interruption that causes us to respond with joy. Think of Christ who, after a long, hard day of ministry and travel, sat wearied by the well in Sychar. Suddenly his season of recovery and rest was interrupted by a woman of Samaria. He had every reason to refuse to let her interrupt His well-deserved rest. First, she was a woman, and rabbis had little or nothing to do with women, particularly in public. On top of that, she was a woman of Samaria. She was of the *other kind*. The Samaritans and the Jews had little to do with each other, and the political, ethnic, religious, and cultural polarization was deeply ingrained in their histories. In addition, she was an immoral woman.

What I find instructive, however, is that Jesus Christ knew that the most important thing was the destiny of her soul, and He surrendered to the interruption to reach out one more time to one more person and seek to bring her to a knowledge of Himself.

This was obviously an option His disciples would never have dreamed of, for when they returned they marveled that He would be speaking with a woman. When they saw the woman, they saw all the barriers of tradition, convention, prejudice, and pride. When Christ saw the woman He saw the harvest. That's an option to many of the interruptions in our lives that is new and significantly strategic.

Not only does God's perspective on interruptions provide new options of response, but His perspective also brings a *new interpretation* to the moment. Note that the angel gave Joseph a unique interpretation of the interruption that had so dramatically affected his life. In the end of verse 20, he told him, "What is conceived in her is from the Holy Spirit."

God is saying, "Joseph, this interruption is not a disaster; this is divine." What from Joseph's perspective was a disaster was really a divine act. It was of God.

What Joseph learns is that the Holy Spirit has done this. And this perspective provides confidence and courage to accept it as a good work of God in his life. Also, God expands his perspectives by giving him a new orientation.

Notice that the angel goes on to say, "You are to give him the name

Jesus, because he will save his people from their sins" (Matthew 1:21).

Matthew says, "All this took place to fulfill what the Lord had said through the prophet [Isaiah]: 'The virgin will be with child and will give birth to a son, and they will call him Immanuel'—which means 'God with us'" (Matthew 1:22–23).

Notice what has happened to Joseph. He is no longer facing a personal disaster. With this new perspective he is given an orientation to realities beyond himself, beyond his own boundaries of the here and now.

When I face a personal interruption, I tend to look at my life in this little box of what is happening right now. We instinctively deal with situations in light of our immediate needs and feelings. That is all we can see. What God did, in coming to Joseph, was to break out the sides of the box and say, "Joseph, look back. You are a significant part of a whole train of divine history that started with the prophets long ago. Not only that, but there will be centuries, generations of people, who will be saved from their sins through this interruption in your life."

You and I sit here today, two thousand years later, redeemed. Hell has been canceled and heaven guaranteed, because of this interruption in Joseph's life. Through this expanded perspective, God gives Joseph an orientation that extended the meaning of the situation far beyond his own immediate circumstances.

Does it ever dawn on us that when God interrupts our lives, He may be doing something that will benefit our children? Or our children's children? What happens in our lives at this moment may affect a far greater sphere than the narrow interests of our own lives. Our actions, our responses to life's situations, may result in something far beyond ourselves and far beyond our expectations.

Joseph's response to the situation would have incredible repercussions. His compassion toward Mary, his response to this Child, would impact generations to come.

Trusting Our Father

Why is it then that we confine ourselves to the tyranny of the moment? We know that our God is the God of the bigger picture. He is the Creator of a divine plan. He comes along and interrupts our lives to cast us as players in a much bigger, much broader, far more significant strategy than the smallness of our immediate situation. Yet, we are so often in bondage to the moments of our lives that we are unable to recog-

a matter of perspective our life or the life God has given! A gift!!!

nize the movement of a bigger, more purposeful God.

Missionary and author Elisabeth Elliot tells the story of how she and her son-in-law took her eighteen-month-old grandson Walter and drove over to the nearest automatic car wash.

This was the first time little Walter had been to a car wash. As the car moved into the machine and the brushes began to whir, the little boy's eyes grew bigger. He would glance at the rushing water and the roaring brushes, and then turn anxiously to look at his father.

Elisabeth says, "He was too small to understand what it was all about, and he'd had no explanation beforehand. What he did know was that Daddy would take care of him."

As the hot air began to blast and the car slowly crept out into the bright sunshine, young Walter's face was lit by a smile. "Everything was okay," says Elisabeth. "Daddy knew what he was doing after all. Like Walter, I have been through some dark tunnels. Although they were frightening, in the end I've found my Heavenly Father always knows the way out."[4]

Our Father knows. He is beside us through the trip. And, even when we don't understand the crashing water and roaring sounds that threaten to overwhelm us, He sees the bigger picture and promises to guide us securely through and accomplish purposes that are far beyond ourselves.

Elisabeth reminds us, "He is not only the Almighty. He is also our Father, and what a father does is not by any means always understood by the child."

What Is God Doing?

Proverbs 3:5–6 affirms the principle: "Trust in the Lord with all your heart and lean not on your own understanding; in all your ways acknowledge him, and he will make your paths straight."

An old hymn repeats the idea of trusting God for the best guidance: "Trust and obey. For there's no other way, to be happy in Jesus, but to trust and obey."

Those words are easy to sing, easy to lean on when life is turning out as we expect it to. But can we trust during difficult circumstances? Can we trust in our heavenly Father when life's problems threaten to overcome us? Can we, like Joseph, trust in an answer that is beyond our comprehension? Do we really believe that "all things work together for good for those who love God and who live according to His purpose"?

Yet that is what we are asked to do. We are to trust not in ourselves, not in our circumstances, but in God and in His divine perspectives.

I am reminded of Corrie ten Boom's story, which was dramatically captured in the film *The Hiding Place*.[5]

As a young woman, Corrie and her family faced the horrors of the concentration camps after hiding Jews from Nazi police. Certainly, World War II and the resulting Holocaust could be listed among life's most devastating interruptions.

Corrie and her sister Betsie were taken to a work camp with thousands of other women. Forced to work at hard labor from daybreak late into the night, they would fall onto their hard, wooden bunks exhausted beyond belief.

How could this desperate situation be used of God?

Then the sisters discovered that the thin mats on which they slept were completely infested with fleas. Betsie thanked God for the fleas, to Corrie's horror. Corrie protested, "He doesn't expect thanks for this."

But Betsie insisted, "There has to be a plan, Corrie." Sure enough, what the sisters did not realize was that God was using those fleas for His divine purpose, a purpose not immediately apparent to those looking through earthly lenses.

As Corrie tells it, she found out only later that the prison guards, repulsed by the fleas, refused to enter the barracks. And, in that flea-infested space, the women found peace and quiet and the freedom to hold Bible studies unhindered by the prison guards.

God used those fleas, those unwelcome, interrupting pests, for His divine purpose.

In life's interruptions, God is doing something above and beyond ourselves and our immediate circumstances. When we look at life from His orientation, what seem like simple interruptions become dramatic turning points that give shape and meaning to His grand plans and our future.

John Sammis's hymn, *Trust and Obey*, speaks to our heart:

> When we walk with the Lord
> In the light of His Word,
> What a glory He sheds on our way!
> While we do His good will,
> He abides with us still,
> and with all who will
>   trust and obey.[6]

The Right Stuff

What does it take to turn the interruptions of our lives into God's intended purposes?

It requires being a special kind of person: a person who is righteous and compassionate. Like Joseph on the road to Bethlehem, like Corrie ten Boom in the concentration camp, we must be surrendered, fully surrendered, to God and His divine purpose in our lives—even when we do not understand what that purpose may be.

In Matthew 1:24, we see Joseph's response to this devastating interruption. "When Joseph woke up, he did what the angel of the Lord had commanded him and took Mary home as his wife." What did Joseph do in the face of these devastating circumstances? He surrendered to the interruption.

When was the last time you surrendered to an interruption? Our interruptions that seem so disruptive and devastating are God's unexpected opportunities to be used of Him for purposes far beyond ourselves. If we really believed that, we'd want to have a couple of interruptions every once in a while.

But to maximize the moment, we must be like Joseph, who was the right kind of person, embracing God's perspective and responding in unqualified surrender.

In 1913, in the small southern town of Tuskegee, Alabama, Rosa Louise McCauley was born.[7] As a black girl growing up in the South, Rosa was limited by her circumstances, yet her parents believed in education and in the Bible. As a child, she learned to trust in God and not to be afraid.

In 1932, Rosa married Raymond Parks. He supported his wife's desire to complete her education, and in 1934 Rosa graduated from high school. She was calm, committed, and strong. What she did not know is that a simple interruption to her ordinary schedule would change her life and alter the course of American history.

One cool December evening in 1955, Rosa headed home from work. She boarded a bus in what was then the usual manner for a woman of her race. She paid at the front of the bus, then re-entered through the back door and found a seat at the rear of the bus.

After she was seated, a white man boarded the bus. The driver, looking back toward Rosa, said, "Let me have those seats." As Rosa says, "It did not seem proper, particularly for a woman to give her seat to a man. All the passengers paid ten cents, just as he did."

When more passengers boarded the bus, the driver again asked Rosa to move, although she was seated in the section allocated to blacks.

Instead of moving, Rosa stayed in her seat, moving closer to the window.

"I do not remember being frightened," said Rosa. "I knew someone had to take the first step. So I made up my mind not to move." In less than five minutes, the police came and arrested Rosa Parks.

Says Rosa, "I did not get on the bus to get arrested; I got on the bus to go home. Getting arrested was one of the worst days in my life. It was not a happy experience. Since I have always been a strong believer in God, I knew that He was with me, and only He could get me through the next step."

This was an ordinary woman with ordinary concerns. She was probably anxious to get home after a long day of work. She was probably wondering what to fix for supper, contemplating which household chores needed to be completed. Certainly the last thing on her mind was to change the course of race relations for our country.

But Rosa Parks was also a woman well-grounded in God's Word. She had been taught to trust God and to believe that His righteousness would prevail. She had a quiet, inner strength that enabled her to survive life's difficulties.

In Rosa's quiet, steadfast way, she allowed an unwelcome interruption in her life to be used for a purpose far greater than her own immediate circumstances. Stepping onto a bus after an ordinary workday changed her life.

Making Sense of Life's Interruptions

What about you and me? Are we willing to change the course of history? Will we allow our lives to be interrupted to serve God's purpose, a purpose far beyond our immediate circumstances? It is only with a perspective like that that we will survive life's crisis moments.

The psalmist David knew what it meant to be led on a detour. Here was a young man with bright promise. Selected by a prophet to be the next king of Israel, he had been given the prospect of an unexpectedly wonderful future. Yet, his road to kingship would not be without its challenging interruptions. Facing a giant, chased by the king, running for his life—I am certain that he must have wondered: *God, where are You taking me?*

But God had purposes in these unsettling interruptions on his way to the throne in Jerusalem. David was a shepherd boy. Although valiant in protecting sheep, he had no military experience, which was indispensable if you were to be a king in his day. So God made him a fugitive, to be chased by Saul and his armies. God gave him a small band of discontented men to garner as the troops that would protect his life. He learned military leadership. He hid in the wilderness and in the caves of Israel. This later would be of strategic importance in terms of his awareness of the terrain as commander-in-chief of the armies of Israel. And he would learn to trust God in everything. All of these indispensable qualities could only be taught to him through a sequence of interruptions that otherwise made no sense at all.

David willingly and with a good spirit surrendered to the interruptions, and God used the interruptions to prepare him to be Israel's greatest king and leader.

God's plans are bigger than ours. Someone once explained that God's plan for our life is like a beautiful needlework tapestry. If you look at the tapestry from below, it is a jumble of knots and tangled thread. But viewed from above—from the proper perspective—the threads combine to create a beautiful picture. It is like that with our lives. Events that we, through our earth-bound lenses, see as unexpected detours are often used by God to lead to even better destinations.

In Psalm 32, verses 8 through 11, God answers the psalmist's fears:

I will instruct you and teach you
in the way you should go;
I will counsel you and watch
  over you.
Do not be like the horse or
  the mule,
which have no understanding
but must be controlled by bit
  and bridle
or they will not come to you.
Many are the woes of the wicked,
but the Lord's unfailing love
surrounds the man who trusts
  in him.
Rejoice in the Lord and be glad,
  you righteous;
sing, all you who are upright
  in heart!

Are we willing to learn? Are we willing to take risks? Do we trust the One who leads us?

Whether the interruption we face is as simple as changing our seats on an airplane, or as difficult and complex as facing death or fighting for survival, we must be ready and prepared to accept life's interruptions in the context of God's intended purpose.

In January of 1996, a blizzard swept from New York to Boston, dumping two to three feet of snow. This was an interruption of the hugest proportions.

News reports showed just how drastically the blizzard immobilized the East Coast. Cars could not maneuver down the street. Motorists simply locked their car doors and abandoned their vehicles by the side of the roads. Schools and businesses closed down. Grocery stores experienced a shortage of food supplies. They called it the worst blizzard since 1979.

The snowstorm was so bad that in Washington, D.C., the president canceled all of his appointments. In New York, the stock market closed trading.

But even six inches of snow can be an interruption. If you've ever lived in the Midwest, you know what it's like to get "dumped on" by the white, fluffy stuff. Looking out the office window, seeing the huge flakes heading downward, you begin to dread the drive home. Even worse is the thought of going home to shovel.

The snow interrupts our lives. Mothers search the house for missing gloves and scarves, bundling up their children. Cars need to be scraped. Sidewalks need salting. Certainly the last thing you want to do after a long day's work is to shovel a sixty-foot-long driveway filled with wet, heavy, dripping snow.

So, you bundle up in gloves, hat, and boots and head out the door. Grumbling and muttering, you grab a shovel and start to work. Your progress is slow but steady. Little by little you work your way down the long driveway.

It is quiet out in the snow. In the dark stillness, there is only the snowy driveway, yourself, and the constant scraping of your shovel. A few stray flakes wind their way down to the pavement.

You pause for a moment to take a deep breath, to rest.

And, in that moment, you begin to see the hand of God.

This snow, this invasion of your life, this unwanted interruption of your schedule, is in itself a gift from God.

How long has it been since you looked forward to a really good snow? How long was it since you made a snowball, threw yourself onto the ground and created a snow angel, grabbed a sled and ran to the nearest hill?

As children, we have time for interruptions. We even anticipate them. We are more willing to see the best in things.

As adults, we are far more reluctant. Our lives are too crowded, too hurried. There is no time for these unscheduled events. We have less patience and even less vision.

But, in and through and despite life's interruptions, God can work miracles. He does work miracles.

Through unexpected events which seem to interfere with our carefully laid plans, God blankets the world with His divine plan. And, in doing so, He creates a thing of holiness and beauty.

The world teaches us to deal with life's interruptions by bracing for the worst and then picking up the pieces in the refuge of a therapist's office. We are so afraid of change, so afraid of interruptions, so afraid of a crack in our carefully constructed armor, that we won't, we cannot, let down our guard.

That is not how we, as believers, are to live.

In his book *The Sacred Journey*, Frederick Buechner describes our resistance to seeing life's interruptions from an eternal perspective.

> To do for yourself the best that you have it in you to do—to grit your teeth and clench your fists in order to survive the world at its harshest and worst—is, by that very act, to be unable to let something be done for you and in you that is more wonderful still.
>
> The trouble with steeling yourself against the harshness of reality is that the same steel that secures your life against being destroyed secures your life also against being opened up and transformed by the

holy power that life itself comes from.[8]

We cannot fool ourselves into thinking that this is all there is. We must do more than simply grit our teeth, clench our fists, and fight for personal survival. For, when we do so, we are limiting God and denying the truth that is in us.

That Which is Unseen

In his second letter to the Corinthians, Paul writes: "So we fix our eyes not on what is seen, but on what is unseen. For what is seen is temporary, but what is unseen is eternal" (2 Corinthians 4:18).

Paul's words speak of an important truth, a truth that helps us deal with the earthly interruptions we so often face. Very often, it is not a matter of changing our situation (which may be completely out of our control), but changing our focus.

We are told not to focus on what is "seen." What does that mean? Well, our natural, human response is to focus on the problem, the evidence at hand. We want to roll up our sleeves, get to work, and solve the problem on our own.

But we are dealing with what we can "see." Paul pushes us away from that focus. Joseph was instructed not to focus on Mary's pregnancy as a single woman. Job was reminded not to focus on his aches and pains and loneliness. Noah was not to focus on the earthly overwhelming task of building an oversized boat. Those were things they could see. Those seen objects did not reveal God's purpose. Those "seen" things were only temporary.

What we are to focus on is that which is "unseen." We are to practice looking at that which is eternal. After all, Scripture tells us, "Faith is being sure of what we hope for and certain of what we do not see" (Hebrews 11:1).

Fixing Our Hearts
on Things Above

In a letter to the church at Colosse, Paul writes, "Since, then, you have been raised with Christ, set your hearts on things above, where Christ is seated at the right hand of God. Set your minds on things above, not on earthly things" (Colossians 3:1–2).

When interruptions happen, we are not to sink into the here and now. We are to focus, to concentrate on "things above." I think of the snow, falling thickly on the ground. We can look at the mess it is creating, the obstacle it is developing in our life. Or, we can look heavenward and praise the Creator of this miracle.

Will these snow days be inter-ruptions to our carefully planned, scheduled lives? Or opportunities to slow down, to focus on things above, to spend time with our children, to read God's Word, to dwell on those things which are truly important in life?

Fixing our hearts on things above means being willing to follow wherever God leads. But it also means that when the road comes to a dead end, when we hit the first road-block, we are not to look earthward in self-pity and frustration. It is then that we must turn heavenward, ready and anxious to undertake His divine-ly guided interruptions.

> Therefore, since we are sur-rounded by such a great cloud of witnesses, let us throw off every-thing that hinders and the sin that so easily entangles, and let us run with perseverance the race marked out for us.

> Let us fix our eyes on Jesus, the author and perfecter of our faith, who for the joy set before him endured the cross, scorning its shame, and sat down at the right hand of the throne of God (Hebrews 12:1–2).

As I stood on the sidewalk out-side our gym, students began to be released one by one, then the staff, then the faculty member who was held as a human shield. Needless to say, we breathed a deep and grateful sigh of relief. Then I saw the police force lead this man handcuffed to the police wagon.

At this point the details of what had happened began to unfold for those of us who had watched from a distance. This man had walked up to the information desk and demanded that a local television station be brought in for him to air his complaints before all of Chicago. He said that he was armed (he actually was not) and that if his demands weren't met, he would shoot anyone in sight. As he then took hostages of the staff and a class that was just dismissing, he held them in the face of the police force who stood at rifle length away from him in the lobby.

In the midst of this, one of our students seated on the floor raised his hand to get the man's attention. He asked if he might pray with him. The man looked startled and said, "That would be good. I need your prayers." The student prayed. Then another prayed, and then another. Then he began releasing the individual students as they prayed.

Through all of this, the faculty member who was being held as the shield and a staff member standing next to him told this man the fact that God really loved him and that although he had come to our campus meaning harm, that God had really brought him here to hear the good news that Jesus Christ cared for him and could not only save his life but could help him in his present circumstances. The staff member took him through the whole plan of salvation step by step.

This was turning out to be one of the most unique evangelistic endeavors ever to take place on our campus. Apparently at gunpoint and in the midst of what would normally be devastating trauma, courageous and confident people were getting beyond the devastating nature of their own interruption to care for the soul of the one who had caused this unwelcome interruption in their lives. I'm confident that the police officers who had been involved in many situations similar to this had never been in quite this kind of setting before.

I think of the witness in the hearts of these policemen as they saw a dramatically different response to one of life's most challenging moments.

That night I sat in my living room and watched the evening news as the major channels in Chicago reported on the event. Over and over again I heard the reporters say that the students of Moody Bible Institute prayed for this one who had taken them hostage. What a resounding affirmation of the difference that Jesus Christ makes in our lives before a watching world!

In chapel on the following day we took the opportunity to put this into a biblical perspective. The incident reinforced the fact that although you can take every possible measure to be safe and secure, there are no safe places in this world. And it further underscored the reality that God has not called us to safety but to service. And that many of God's finest people throughout history have been willing to serve Christ in the face of great danger. In fact, it seemed clear to me that this was a teaching and training moment for these fine students on our campus, to teach them to be willing to maintain their confidence, courage, and commitment to Christ in the midst of deep crisis.

God obviously had permitted this to happen in spite of our well-trained campus security, to enable us to do something above and beyond ourselves that otherwise could not have happened. Our students continue to work with this man who has since been incarcerated. We are praying that the ultimate purpose in this interruption is that he will share eternity with us in glory.

How do we handle life's interruptions? By fixing our eyes not on our problems, but on our Lord and Savior Jesus Christ, who endured for us the greatest interruption of them all. In Him and through Him we can realize that this life is not all there is. Looking heavenward, we will find the courage to respond with righteousness and compassion, a willingness to surrender, and a divine perspective that provides new options, new interruptions, and a new orientation. To us living will mean faithfully waiting for God to do something above and beyond ourselves.

Notes

1. Geisel, Theodore S., *Oh, the Places You'll Go!* (New York: Random House, 1990). Reprinted by permission.

2. Smith, Hannah Whitall, *The Christian's Secret of a Happy Life* (Waco, Tex.: Word, 1984).

3. Wangerin, Walter, "A Stranger in Joseph's House," *Christianity Today,* 11 December 1995.

4. Elliot, Elisabeth, *On Asking God Why* (Old Tappan, N.J.: Fleming Revell, 1989).

5. The movie (World Wide Pictures, 1975) is based on Corrie ten Boom's book *The Hiding Place.*

6. Sammis, John, "Trust and Obey."

7. Parks, Rosa, with Gregory J. Reed, *Quiet Strength* (Grand Rapids: Zondervan, 1994).

8. Buechner, Frederick, *The Sacred Journey* (New York: Harper and Row, 1982).

Moody Press, a ministry of the Moody Bible
Institute, is designed for education, evangeliza-
tion, and edification. If we may assist you in
knowing more about Christ and the Christian Life,
please write us without obligation:
Moody Press, c/o MLM, Chicago, Illinois 60610.